Edward Cline

ISLAM'S REIGN OF TERROR

Voltaire Press

Library of Congress Cataloguing-in-Publication Data

Edward Cline (1946 -)
Islam's Reign of Terror/Edward Cline

ISBN-13: 978-1500920777
ISBN-10: 1500920770
ASIN: B00MXG2SZO

Voltaire Press
Durham, North Carolina

Publisher's Note: The author and Voltaire Press have made every effort to ensure the accuracy of the information contained herein.

Table of Contents

ISLAM'S REIGN OF TERROR

ISLAMIC TERRORISM IN AMERICA

On Monday, April 15, 2013, during the Boston Marathon, two bombs exploded among spectators near the finish line on Boylston Avenue. Three people, including an eight-year-old boy, were killed, and over two hundred injured, many losing their legs and suffering wounds caused by nails, ball bearings and other shrapnel.

During the week, photographs from surveillance cameras showed a number of candidates who might have planted the bombs, which were improvised explosive devices (IEDs) fashioned with common kitchen pressure cookers, of a kind that took so many American lives in Iraq and Afghanistan. Then it began to dawn on the mainstream media and the authorities that the bombs were planted by Muslim *jihadists*.

The murderers were brothers, Dzhokhar A. Tsarnaev, 19, and Tamerlan Tsarnaev, 26 – two young Muslims whose parents brought them to America from the war-torn Russian province of Chechnya. The Tsarnaev brothers had lived in the Boston area for ten years. Their parents had returned to Russia. The younger brother, Dzhokhar, was a naturalized American citizen. The older brother, Tamerlan, might have been granted citizenship, except that in 2009 he had beaten his American girlfriend, Nadine Ascencao.[1]

Tamerlan was killed during a fire-fight with authorities. Dzhokhar was located at the end of the week, wounded, hiding in a resident's covered boat in Watertown outside Boston. He was arrested, hospitalized, and initially charged with possessing and using a WMD (weapon of mass destruction).

The Boston Marathon bombing is the latest episode of violent Islamic *jihad*. But what is *jihad*? In Islam, it has two meanings: the self-generated "struggle" (*fitna*) a devout Muslim is obligated to undergo to become a "good" Muslim; and to wage war on non-believers of Islam to convert them to Islam, or to subjugate them, or to kill them.[2]

Islamic terrorists choose the latter form of "struggle." The fact, however, is that *fitna* encompasses *both* meanings, with terrorists embodying, practicing, and fulfilling the fundamental essence of Islam. Most Muslims are "passive," that is, they are seen to not practice their religion to the fullest, and so are not consistent in living according to Islam's fundamental tenets. They are "Friday-go-to-mosque" Muslims, despised by Islamic clerics here and abroad who preach violent *jihad,* and by the terrorists themselves.

This is eminently underscored by the fact that Muslims as well as non-believers have been the victims of terrorist violence, in either indiscriminate suicide bombings targeting Westerners, or in the interminable conflicts among various sects of Islam. According to an Al Arabiya News item of September 11, 2011, twenty-eight Muslims of various sects were among the casualties on 9/11/2001 when planes struck the World Trade Center, including three in two of the hijacked planes. The Washington Post reported on February 23, 2006, that Sunni "extremists" bombed a giant Shi'ite mosque in Samara, north of Baghdad.

More recently, Reuters on January 23, 2013, reported that a Sunni suicide bomber killed twenty-two Shi'ites during a funeral inside a mosque in Tuz Khurmato, Iraq. While both Sunnis and Shi'ites regard the *Koran* as divine and untouchable, their conflict centers on who succeeded Mohammad as the spiritual leader of Islam, and also on differing interpretations of the *Hadith* and Sharia law.

Nevertheless, to be wholly consistent with the tenets of Islam and to express one's unconditional faith in it, a Muslim must be willing to die to advance the spread of Islam, and be deemed a "martyr" for it or a self-sacrificing "warrior" (*Mujaheddin*).

Fox News reports that Tamerlan Tsarnaev sent his mother text messages saying that he was willing to die for Islam's cause.[3] His mother, Zubeidat Tsarnaeva, interviewed in Russia, ranted against the U.S., saying she did not care if both of her sons were killed, and that she did not care, either, if she died advancing Islam.[4]

Globally, incidents of Islamic terrorism since 9/11 alone have passed the 20,000 mark. Islam has been at war with the West, and in particularly with the U.S. and Israel, for decades, if one does not count the centuries Muslims have raided European coasts for slaves, estimated to be around two million, and captured American merchant vessels in the 18th and early 19th centuries, and enslaved their crews or held them for ransom. The U.S. has been the subject of dozens of attacks here and abroad. Some of these are listed below.

Two kinds of *jihad* or terrorism have been committed: direct violence which employed force to kill and destroy; and indirect *jihad*, which threatens the use of force, such as occurred when images of Mohammad or books or papers critical of Islam were published or were about to be published, and the publishers and authors threatened with violence or with lawsuits by Muslims (colloquially called "lawfare").

Almost simultaneously with the Boston Marathon bombings, *The Telegraph* (London) reported that Canadian authorities announced the arrest of two Canadian Muslims who were plotting to wreck with as many casualties as possible a train link between Toronto and New York City.

> Chief Supt Strachan, from the Royal Canadian Mounted Police, said that Chiheb Esseghaier and Raed Jaser, who live in the Montreal and Toronto areas, were conspiring to carry out an attack against Via Rail, but posed no immediate threat. "It was definitely in the planning stage but not imminent," she told reporters.[5]

The following is a partial timeline of Islamic terrorist actions, culled from Voltaire Press's *Muhammad: The Banned Images*, and other sources, beginning in 1955. The timeline omits the numerous and bloody Islamic terrorist plane hijackings that began in the late 1960s:

1955 – April: Eight-foot sculpture on the Appellate Division of the First Department of the New York State Supreme Court (at Madison Square Park), in place since ca. 1900, is identified during renovation as Muhammad, and removed after the Egyptian, Indonesian and Pakistani ambassadors to the United Nations protest its presence.

1979 – November. 4: Tehran, Iran: Iranian radical students seized the U.S. embassy, taking 66 hostages. 14 were later released. The remaining 52 were freed after 444 days on the day of President Reagan's inauguration.

1982 –1991: Lebanon: Thirty U.S. and other Western hostages kidnapped in Lebanon by Hezbollah. Some were killed, some died in captivity, and some were eventually released. Briton Terry Anderson was held for 2,454 days.

1983 – April 18, Beirut, Lebanon: U.S. embassy destroyed in suicide car-bomb attack; 63 dead, including 17 Americans. The Islamic Jihad claimed responsibility.

1983 – October 23, Beirut, Lebanon: Shi'ite suicide bombers exploded a truck near U.S. military barracks at Beirut airport, killing 241 marines. Minutes later a second bomb killed 58 French paratroopers in their barracks in West Beirut

1983 – Dec. 12, Kuwait City, Kuwait: Shi'ite truck bombers attacked the U.S. embassy and other targets, killing 5 and injuring 80

1984 – September 20, east Beirut, Lebanon: Truck bomb exploded outside the U.S. embassy annex, killing 24, including 2 U.S. military

1984 – Dec. 3, Beirut, Lebanon: Kuwait Airways Flight 221, from Kuwait to Pakistan, hijacked and diverted to Tehran. 2 Americans killed

1985 – April 12, Madrid, Spain: Bombing at restaurant frequented by U.S. soldiers, killed 18 Spaniards and injured 82

1985 – June 14, Beirut, Lebanon: TWA Flight 847 en route from Athens to Rome hijacked to Beirut by Hezbollah terrorists and held for 17 days. A U.S. Navy diver executed.

1985 – October 7, Mediterranean Sea: Gunmen attack Italian cruise ship, *Achille Lauro*. One U.S. tourist killed. Hijacking linked to Libya

1985 – December 18, Rome, Italy, and Vienna, Austria: Airports in Rome and Vienna were bombed, killing 20 people, 5 of whom were Americans. Bombing linked to Libya

1986 – April 2, Athens, Greece: A bomb exploded aboard TWA flight 840 en route from Rome to Athens, killing 4 Americans and injuring 9

1986 – April 5, West Berlin, Germany: Libyans bombed a disco frequented by U.S. servicemen, killing 2 and injuring hundreds

1988 – December 21, Lockerbie, Scotland: N.Y.-bound Pan-Am Boeing 747 exploded in flight from a terrorist bomb and crashed into Scottish village, killing all 259 aboard and 11 on the ground. Passengers included 35 Syracuse University students and many U.S. military personnel. Libya formally admitted responsibility 15 years later (Aug. 2003) and offered $2.7 billion compensation to victims' families.

1989 – February 14: Ayatollah Ruhollah Khomeini issues fatwa against Salman Rushdie over *The Satanic Verses*, a fictional and often comedic account of Islam.

1989 – March 1: Cody's Books and a branch of Waldenbooks in Berkeley, CA, are firebombed after their managers assert that they will continue to sell *The Satanic Verses*

1989 – April: Collets and Dillons in London are firebombed for stocking *The Satanic Verses*; bombs also at High Wycombe, on London's King's Road, in the Liberty department store, and the York Penguin bookshop. Unexploded devices discovered at Nottingham, Guildford, and Peterborough

1989– August 3: Unidentified 21-year-old Lebanese man dies priming a book bomb he intended to use to kill Rushdie

1991– July 3: Ettore Capriolo, the Italian translator of *The Satanic Verses*, is beaten and stabbed in Milan, after death threats by Muslims

1991– July 12: Hitoshi Igarashi, professor of comparative culture and Japanese translator of *The Satanic Verses*, is stabbed to death at Tsukuba University, near Tokyo

1993 – July 2: Attack targeting Aziz Nesin, a translator of *The Satanic Verses*, kills 37 Alewi intellectuals at the Madimak Hotel in Sivas, Turkey

1993 – October 12: William Nygaard, publisher of *The Satanic Verses* in Norway, is shot and injured

Radio Free Europe/Radio Liberty, in September 2012, reported that the fatwa on Rushdie stands, with an increase in the bounty on his head. Ever since 1988, he has had to live in hiding and goes about with a bodyguard.

> Reports from Iran say a semiofficial religious group, 15 Khordad Foundation, has increased to $3.3 million the bounty on the life of British author Salman Rushdie. The news comes more than 23 years after the fatwa, or religious edict, was issued by Iranian Supreme Leader Ayatollah Ruhollah Khomeini for what he labeled blasphemy in the novel "The Satanic Verses." The latest call to kill the novelist comes against a backdrop of global Muslim outrage over a low-budget film made in the U.S. that impugns the Prophet Muhammad.

1997 – Council on American-Islamic Relations (CAIR) objects to the figure of Muhammad in Adolf Weinman's frieze of lawmakers in the Supreme Court, Washington, D.C. Chief Justice Rehnquist replies that

it is unlawful to remove or injure any architectural feature of the Supreme Court, but that the Supreme Court will change its tourist literature to be more sensitive to Muslim religious beliefs.

2001 – September 11: In a coordinated attack on the U.S., two passenger planes hijacked by Muslim *jihadists* slam into the World Trade Center in New York City. The buildings collapse, killing over 2,000 people. Another hijacked plane is crashed into the Pentagon in Washington D.C. A fourth plane plunges into an empty field in Shanksville, PA, when passengers attempt to wrest control of it from its Muslim hijackers. This plane was thought to be targeting either the White House or the Capitol Building in Washington D.C. In all, nearly 3,000 people are killed in the attacks, more than the casualties of the Japanese attack on Pearl Harbor (2,402 dead).

2004 – November 2: Theo van Gogh, filmmaker, is murdered by Mohammed Bouyeri, a Dutch Moroccan. Van Gogh's film *Submission* was "intended to provoke discussion on the position of enslaved Muslim women... directed at the fanatics, the fundamentalists." Bouyeri shot van Gogh twice, slit his throat, and used the knife to attach a note to van Gogh's chest that threatened the life of Ayaan Hirsi Ali (scriptwriter for Submission and former member of the Dutch Parliament). Hirsi Ali said, "I absolutely wish that Theo had not been killed. But I don't regret that I made it. In fact, I'm proud of that film. To feel otherwise would be to deny everything I stand for."

2005 – September 30: Flemming Rose, culture editor of Jyllands-Posten, another Danish newspaper, publishes 12 cartoon renderings of Muhammad. (See *Muhammad: The "Banned" Images*, pp. 6-7 and no. 30, with a translation of the text explaining why the cartoons were commissioned and published.)

2005 – December: Voltaire's *Mahomet* (written in 1741; see *Muhammad: The "Banned" Images,* pp. 12 and 22) is given a public reading in Saint-Genis-Pouilly, France, despite the fact that Muslims in the town state that the play "constitutes an insult to the entire Muslim community" and demand the reading be cancelled "in order to preserve peace." Mayor Hubert Bertrand responds that the French constitution guarantees free speech. On the night of the performance, minor disturbances erupt outside the theater, but Bertrand states afterward that he is proud his town refused to cave in to pressure: "For a long time we have not confirmed our convictions, so lots of people think they can contest them."

Here is the West's response to the Danish Mohammad cartoons. Nothing much has changed. The West refuses to acknowledge Islam as an enemy:

2006 – January 30: Former President Bill Clinton, speaking in Qatar of the Danish cartoons: "None of us are totally free of stereotypes about people of different races, different ethnic groups, and different religions ... there was this appalling example in northern Europe, in Denmark ... these totally outrageous cartoons against Islam."

2006 – February 3: Kurtis Cooper, spokesman for the U.S. State Department, announces: "We all fully recognize and respect freedom of the press and expression but it must be coupled with press responsibility. Inciting religious or ethnic hatreds in this manner is not acceptable."

2006 – February 3: British Foreign Secretary Jack Straw, on the Danish cartoons: "I believe that the republication of these cartoons has been unnecessary. It has been insensitive. It has been disrespectful and it has been wrong."

2006 – February 4: Demonstrations, protests, and firebombings in Syria, Denmark, Gaza Strip

2006 – February 5: Demonstrations, protests, and firebombings in Lebanon

2006 – February 6: Demonstrations, protests, and firebombings in Afghanistan, Iran, Indonesia, Somalia, United Arab Emirates

The New York Times, apparently oblivious to the fact that in the U.S., it has the freedom to publish its wisdom, bias or ignorance without fear of recrimination or force, went on record against freedom of speech:

2006 – February 7: *The New York Times* states, "The New York Times and much of the rest of the nation's news media have reported on the cartoons but refrained from showing them. That seems a reasonable choice for news organizations that usually refrain from gratuitous assaults on religious symbols, especially since the cartoons are so easy to describe in words."

2006 – February 17: Two editors of the University of Illinois' student newspaper, the *Daily Illini*, are suspended (one is later fired) for reprinting the cartoons

2006– February 17: Protests in Libya. A Pakistani cleric and a minister of an Indian province offer $1 million to anyone who will kill any of the Danish cartoonists

2006– February 17: Italian Minister Roberto Calderoli appears on TV wearing a T-shirt depicting one of the Danish cartoons. Prime Minister Silvio Berlusconi demands Calderoli's resignation. Calderoli states, "What happened in Libya has nothing to do with my T-shirt. The question is different. What's at stake is Western civilization." He later quits under protest.

2006 – April 1: Borders and Waldenbooks refuse to stock the April/May 2006 issue of Free Inquiry magazine, because it includes the Danish cartoons: "For us, the safety and security of our customers and employees is a top priority, and we believe that carrying this issue could challenge that priority," says a spokeswoman for the Borders

Group. Paul Kurtz, editor in chief of *Free Inquiry*, says, "To refuse to distribute a publication because of fear of vigilante violence is to undermine freedom of press– so vital for our democracy."

2006 – September 17: Pope Benedict XVI apologizes to Muslims twice in two days for quoting (in a discussion of reason vs. violence) a 14th-c. comment by Byzantine emperor Manuel II Paleologus: "Show me just what Muhammad brought that was new, and there you will find things only evil and inhuman, such as his command to spread by the sword the faith he preached."

2006 – September 26: Berlin Opera's production of Mozart's *Idomeneo* is cut short after two performances for fear of Muslim reprisals. Hans Neuenfels had added a scene that involved the decapitated heads of Jesus, Buddha, and Muhammad.

Britain has succumbed to politically correct speech in various realms, but particularly when reporting news about crimes, especially rape, committed by Muslims. Most newspapers, courts, and government entities employ, instead, the euphemism "Asians," or refrain from identifying the criminals' religion or ethnic origins.

2006 – October: London's Whitechapel Gallery removes 12 works by Surrealist Hans Bellmer from an exhibition, for fear that the sexual overtones will be offensive to the Muslim population in the neighborhood

2008 – February 12: Two Tunisians and a Dane are arrested and charged with planning to murder Kurt Westergaard, one of the 12 Danish cartoonists

In **February 2013**, Kurt Westergaard, the famous Norwegian cartoonist and the subject of several assassination attempts by Muslims, was the target of another attempt when a Muslim, posing as a mailman, appeared at his door outside Copenhagen, and tried to shoot him. Westergaard foiled the attempt, and the perpetrator fled. Westergaard was also the subject of a government suit for his "offensive" cartoons. He was acquitted of any wrong-doing.

2008 – March 20: Osama bin Laden releases an audiotape calling the cartoons part of a "new crusade" against Islam, and threatening reprisals against Europeans

2008– March 27: Release of *Fitna* by Geert Wilders, Dutch politician and chair of the Freedom Party; film includes the Danish cartoons and condemns Islamic extremism

2008 – August 12: Random House announces that it will not publish Sherry Jones' *The Jewel of Medina*, a fictional account of the life of one of the wives of Muhammad, because "it could incite acts of violence."

2009 – January 21: Amsterdam Court of Appeals orders *Fitna* filmmaker Geert Wilders prosecuted for the "incitement of hatred and discrimination"

2009 – February 10: Two days before the airing of *Fitna* in the Palace of Westminster, Home Secretary Jacqui Smith bans Wilders from entering the U.K. on grounds that he is an "undesirable person"

2009 – August 12: Yale University Press announces that it will not include any images in Jytte Klausen's *The Cartoons that Changed the World*, a study of the effect of the Danish cartoons. John Donatich, director of YUP, says the decision to withdraw the cartoons was "overwhelming and unanimous," that he does not want "blood on my hands," and that the cartoons are freely available on the Internet and can be accurately described in words, so reprinting them could be interpreted easily as gratuitous.

2009 – October: Two men are arrested in Chicago and charged with terrorism, accused of plotting to murder Flemming Rose, who was responsible for the original publication of the cartoons

2009 – November 5: Army psychiatrist Major Nidal Malik Hasan, a Muslim, kills twelve soldiers and one civilian at Ft. Hood, Texas, shouting "Allahu Akbar!" (Allah is the greatest!)

2009 – November 25: Appearances at Columbia and Princeton by Nonie Darwish, executive director of Former Muslims United and author of *Cruel and Usual Punishment: The Terrifying Global Implications of Islamic Law*, are canceled at the last moment under pressure from Muslim groups on campus

2010 – April: The Comedy Central show "South Park" satirizes Muhammad. Islamists threaten violence. Obama administration does nothing to defend the show's creators, Comedy Central, or free speech.

2010 – September: Molly Norris, the cartoonist who created the protest "Everybody Draw Mohammad Day" on Facebook, is forced into hiding when an Islamic cleric calls for her murder. Facebook removes the site, then reinstates it.

And, closer in time to the Boston Marathon bombings, there were these recent terrorist actions;

2011– January 17, Spokane, Washington: A pipe bomb is discovered along the route of the Martin Luther King, Jr. memorial march. The bomb, a "viable device" set up to spray marchers with shrapnel and to cause multiple casualties, is defused without any injuries.

2011 – June 23: Geert Wilders is acquitted by the Dutch court. He faced five counts of hate speech and discrimination for remarks made publicly between October 2006 and March 2008, and in his controversial short film *Fitna*). Wilders also compared the *Koran* with Adolf Hitler's *Mein Kampf*. Wilders must live and travel under constant bodyguard.

2012– September 11, Benghazi, Libya: Militants armed with antiaircraft weapons and rocket-propelled grenades fire upon the American consulate, killing U.S. ambassador to Libya Christopher

Stevens and three other embassy officials. U.S. Secretary of State Hillary Clinton reluctantly conceded that the U.S. believed that the Islamic Maghreb, a group closely linked to Al Qada, orchestrated the attack. The Obama administration had previously asserted that Al Qada had been defeated, while the State Department had arranged to have the consulate guarded by elements of various *jihadist* organizations.

2013– February 1, Ankara, Turkey: Ecevit Sanli detonates a bomb near a gate at the U.S. Embassy. Sanli dies after detonating the bomb. One Turkish guard is also killed. Didem Tuncay, a respected television journalist, is injured in the blast. Unlike the bombing at the embassy in Benghazi last September, the U.S. government immediately calls the bombing a terrorist attack. According to Turkish officials, the attack is from the Revolutionary People's Liberation Party, which has been labeled a terrorist organization by the U.S. and other nations.

(From "Free Speech at Risk: Murder, Mayhem. and Self-Censorship."[6] Another list of terrorist attacks against and in the U.S., including Islamic terrorist attacks, can be found at Info Please.[7])

A BRIEF HISTORY OF ISLAMIC TERROR

The Roots

Before Mohammad, Islam did not exist. The Arabian Peninsula was a potpourri of pagan religions. Mohammad, the "prophet" of Allah and founder of Islam, was born in 570 A.D. Accounts of his pre-Islamic career variously identify him as a prosperous merchant or a notorious brigand who raided towns and caravans. In 610 he supposedly received his first revelation of the *Koran* (or *Qur'an*) via the angel Gabriel, a messenger of Allah. Other "revelations" followed.

With little success, Mohammad attempted to convert the residents of Mecca to Islam (which means *submission*). He was scorned by the polytheists of that town and more or less banished from Mecca. He and his small band of followers retired to Medina. He returned to Mecca in 624 with an army and conquered it, compelling its residents to accept Islam as the "only one true religion" and Allah as the only God, and ordering the destruction of all pagan idols.

Failing persuasion, Mohammad resorted to the sword. That was the beginning of Islamic *jihad* and terrorism.

Mohammad died in 632. His successors, the Mohammadans, also known as Mahometans, Moslems, or Muslims, even while they were engaged in bloody conflicts over who was Mohammad's true heir, continued his *jihad* until all of the Arabian Peninsula and Armenia were under Islamic rule. In 634 the Muslims invaded Palestine. In 639 they invaded Egypt and took Alexandria. In 642 the first coin bearing a reference to Mohammad appeared. In 711 the Muslims invaded and conquered Spain, but were turned back by the Franks at the battle of Tours in 732 from conquering the rest of Europe.

Obeying the will of Allah and wishing to fulfill the purported prophecy of Mohammad, Constantinople, capital of the Eastern Roman or Byzantine Empire, was unsuccessfully besieged twice by Muslim caliphs, between 674 and 678, and between 717 and 718. When the

Empire collapsed into anarchy, Islam rushed in to fill the vacuum in the Middle East, just as rampaging barbarian Huns and Visigoths filled the vacuum left in Europe by the collapse of the Roman Empire. Constantinople finally fell to the Islamic Ottoman Turks in 1453.

While Europe was embarking on the Renaissance, which would lead to the Enlightenment, the Middle East was falling under the oppressive and regressive rule of Islam, and would reject the Enlightenment. For example, according to the *New World Encyclopedia*, the Enlightenment "advocated reason as a means to establishing an authoritative system of aesthetics, ethics, government, and even religion, which would allow human beings to obtain objective truth about the whole of reality."[8.]

Islam, on the other hand, according to S.H. Nasr in the *Encyclopedia*, spurned the Enlightenment because it separated "knowledge from value. Western science and technology…is immoral [*sic*] because there is no concern with the consequences of progress, but focus only with progress itself. Science no longer serves humanity, but its own quest for yet more knowledge."

> "His basic critique is that reason became detached from "revelation," and thus also from values ….Other Muslims argue that while Western science, post-Enlightenment, places trust in reason alone, Islamic science places its trust in God's revelation; Western science values science for its own sake,

> Islamic science regards itself as a type of worship; Western science claims impartiality, Islamic science claims a partiality towards what is true and beneficial for humanity; Western science reduces the world to what can be empirically verified, Islamic science admits the reality of the spiritual dimension."[9.]

The Ottoman Turks wished to expand their rule in Europe. After conquering the Balkans, they laid siege to Vienna, Austria, gateway to the rest of Europe, twice, in 1529 and 1683. The Ottomans were dealt a decisive defeat in 1683 after failing to capture Vienna. The Turks retired to rule over the Middle East until the Ottomans were defeated in World War I.

Islam was born of violence. It has been spread by violence. Its character is defined by violence. Its history, from the time of Mohammad in the seventh century up to the twenty-first, has been a bloody record of conquest by the spear, by the sword, and now by plane hijackings, automatic weapons, and the bomb. When Islamic *dawa*, or proselytizing, fails to win new converts, it resorts to force, e.g., stoning, arson, beheading, slavery, murder.

And it is by its nature a violent ideology because Islam rejects on principle the only civilized means of settling disputes peacefully: persuasion, debate, discussion, i.e., man's faculty of reason. Islam regards man as a helpless plaything in a chaotic universe ruled by a spiteful, omnipotent, supernatural deity (Allah). The common man must submit to Allah (and his representatives here on Earth) because he is by nature incapable of thinking for himself. Every totalitarian ideology starts by attacking man's faculty of reason.

Islam cannot be anything but violent. Its doctrine prescribes violence, and compels its adherents to employ force, to wage *jihad*. Its "prophet," Mohammad, sanctioned and urged violence. Terrorism is but one of its violent tools, aside from military conquest and the categorical imperative that Muslims and non-Muslims alike submit to the "will of Allah," as adherents or as *dhimmis*, or else meet with death or slavery. The "categorical imperative," an important element in Islamic ethics, is discussed later.

Bill Warner of *Political Islam* notes that:

> Mohammed had little success with Islam until he transformed it into a political system. He preached the religion of Islam in Mecca for thirteen years and made about 150 converts. He left Mecca and moved to Medina. In Medina he turned to politics and *jihad*. In the last nine years of his life, Mohammed was involved in an event of violence on the average of every six

16

weeks. The political method persuaded every Arab to convert to Islam. The religion did not succeed; it was politics that made Islam powerful.[10]

All three main texts of Islam – the *Koran*, the *Hadith* or *Sunna*, and the *Sira* – glorify and sanction violence against unbelievers of all stripes to cause conversion to it, or submission to it, or death. Much is made of the "peaceful" verses in the *Koran*.[11] But later verses abrogated all but a few of those verses with violent ones. It is the later, violent verses that define the *Koran* and its companion documents. The "peaceful" passages in the *Koran* are as irrelevant to Islam's essence as is the fact that Mafia hit men might be "peaceful" at a child's birthday party.

Islam's Origins and Character

Scholars have determined that Islam itself is a mongrel creed that borrowed heavily from Greek, Middle Eastern pagan, Hebrew, and Christian creeds in the first millennium. "Allah" was originally the name of a pagan moon god, one of dozens of other pagan deities of the period.

Above all, Islam is a totalitarian ideology wearing the vestments of a theocratic religion, whose governing law is Sharia. It directs the life of a Muslim in virtually every aspect of his existence, from the number of times he must pray every day, to the number of wives he may have, to his diet, to his relationships with non-believers or "infidels." Because the *Koran* proscribes how and why a Muslim must live, with the authority to enforce conformity codified in Sharia law, there is no dividing line or wall between the religion and the state. Islam *is* the state and Sharia is its constitution.

But what, specifically, is Sharia? Mordechai Kedar and David Yerushalmi, in their summer 2011 *Middle East Quarterly* article, "Sharia and Violence in American Mosques," described Sharia:

> Shari'a is the Islamic system of law based primarily on two sources held by Muslims to be respectively direct revelation from God and divinely inspired: the Qur'an and the Sunna (sayings, actions, and traditions of Muhammad). There are other jurisprudential sources for Shari'a derived from the legal rulings of Islamic scholars. These scholars, in turn, may be adherents of differing schools of Islamic jurisprudence. Notwithstanding those differences, the divergence at the level of actual law is, given the fullness of the *corpus juris,* confined to relatively few marginal issues. Thus, there is general unity and agreement across the Sunni-Shi'ite divide and across the various Sunni *madh'habs* (jurisprudential schools) on core normative behaviors.[12]

For example, a stricter sect of Judaism, such as the Hassidic, also proscribes what a Jew may or may not do. But Judaism, regardless of the sect, is not a belligerent creed seeking to overthrow and replace secular law with the *Torah*. Judaism does not decree universal submission to it. Islam, however, is a Hobson's choice: submit to it, or die, or be enslaved.

In practice, Sharia law is a brutal, primitive system which, among its other barbarities, sanctions the murder of Jews, homosexuals, apostates, and adulterous women (Muslim men are usually exempt from punishment for the latter offense); the genital mutilation of girls and women; the enslavement of infidels, otherwise known as *kaffirs* or *dhimmis*; the collection of a poll tax, or *jizya* (a kind of Mafia-style "protection" money) from non-believers; and the use of force to compel obedience and submission to Islam.

An *Islamist Watch* article of June 21, 2012, cites many of the consequences of full-throttle Sharia law. It carries stories and graphic videos of a Sudanese woman being lashed for some undefined "sexual" offense, of a Saudi woman being harassed by Saudi religious police in a Riyadh shopping mall for wearing nail polish, of a Muslim woman being stoned to death in the Pakistan-Afghanistan frontier, of four homosexuals being hanged in Iran, and the beheading of an apostate in Tunisia for having converted to Christianity (YouTube removed the latter video).[13.]

Islam, a fundamentally misogynist ideology, also condones the rape and even mutilation of "infidel" women who do not wear the *burqa* or *niqab* or otherwise cover their hair, faces and extremities. British and European newspapers are replete with stories of European girls and women being assaulted by gangs of Muslims, who regard "uncovered" women as "raw meat asking to be raped." Lara Logan's account of her assault in Tahir Square, Cairo, on February 11, 2011, is merely the most publicized instance of how Muslims are taught that women are legitimate subjects for criminal assault, especially if they are non-Muslims.[14.]

19

Islam also condones the tribal practice of "honor killing," when a female Muslim "dishonors" the family by becoming "too Western," i.e., when she makes independent choices, for example, about who to marry and what she will wear in public. Islam sanctions the killing of their daughters, cousins, or wives. This barbaric and criminal practice, common in Islamic nations, is on the rise in America and Europe in Muslim communities.

The AHA Foundation, a non-profit group dedicated to eradicating religious or culturally sanctioned violence against western women, cites many instances of honor killings in the U.S. and Canada. In the week of November 16, 2012, it reported:

- In Arizona: Yusra Farhan was convicted and sentenced for tying her 20-year-old daughter to a bed with rope and a padlock and burning her face with a hot spoon when she refused to marry a man nearly 20 years her senior. The girl's father and sister were also arrested for their complicity.

- In California: Kassim Alhimidi was charged with the murder of his wife, Shaima Alawadi. While police initially believed the case to be a hate crime, investigators uncovered the fact that Alhimidi had plans to send his daughter to Iraq to marry a cousin, and that Shaima intended to divorce him. The case is now being characterized as an honor killing.

- In Toronto: Peer Khairi was convicted of second-degree murder in the brutal stabbing death of his wife, Randjida. The trial heard that the killing was honor-based: Khairi was enraged over Randjida's "disobedience" and her acceptance of their children's Western attitudes to clothing and dating.

- In Edmonton: Muhammad Rafi and Najma Khokhar were arrested and charged with assaulting and forcibly confining their 21-year-old daughter after she refused to be taken abroad to submit to a forced marriage.[15.]

These represent a small fraction of such murders in North America. Honor killings in the U.S. and Canada receive little Mainstream Media attention because to report them is perceived as being "Islamophobic" or evidence of bigotry. Only sensational killings are reported. *Fox News* on February 16, 2009, for example, reported the beheading of a Buffalo woman. New end note

> The estranged wife of a Muslim television executive feared for her life after filing for divorce last month from her abusive husband, her attorney said – and was then found beheaded Thursday in his upstate New York television studio. Aasiya Z. Hassan, 37, was found dead on Thursday at the offices of Bridges TV in Orchard Park, N.Y., near Buffalo. Her husband, Muzzammil Hassan, 44, has been charged with second-degree murder.[16.]

Islam in America

On July 4, 1998, Omar Ahmad, founder in 1994 of the Council on American-Islamic Relations (CAIR, an alleged "civil rights" organization, with over thirty chapters in the U.S., but with ties to Hamas, a terrorist organization), said in a speech during a banquet in Fremont, California, that

> "Islam isn't in America to be equal to any other religions, but to become dominant. The Koran, the Muslim book of scripture, should be the highest authority in America, and Islam the only accepted religion on Earth."[17.]

This means that the *Declaration of Independence* and the *United States Constitution*, the secular law of the land, should be replaced by Sharia law and the country governed by Islamic, religious jurisprudence.

Ahmad also said in the same speech:

> "One of the challenges is understanding the totality of Islam. Don't come up with an opinion and find out the things that

support it in Islam. Everything we need to know is in the Koran. We don't need to look somewhere else."

Lisa Gardiner, who reported on Ahmad's July 2ⁿᵈ speech in the *San Ramon Valley Herald* in her July 4, 1998 article, "American Muslim leader urges faithful to spread Islam's message," noted his remarks on the "difficulty" of Muslims assimilating into America's secular society. Ahmad dismissed the notion as moot.

> Muslim institutions, schools, and economic power should be strengthened in America, he said. Those who stay in America should be "open to society without melting (into it)...."

That goes some way to explaining the "difficulties" the Boston bomber brothers, Dzhokhar A. Tsarnaev and Tamerlan Tsarnaev had in assimilating into American society. Their irrational obsession with tribal loyalties in Chechnya and a fascination with the power Islamic *jihad* purportedly would give them, were elements that prevented them from becoming American individuals. So they decided to bomb the American "melting pot" in Boston. If *dawa* fails, resort to other means of "persuasion," such as inflicting death and dismemberment.

The Muslim Brotherhood: The Umbrella Organization

The Muslim Brotherhood, which last year came to power in Egypt, has contributed to the turmoil in North Africa, and is fighting to come to power in Syria. It is the "evil genius" behind much of the violence and terrorism that has bloodied the planet for so many decades. The Brotherhood, founded in 1928 by Hassan al-Banna, has a motto:

> "Allah is our objective. The Prophet is our leader. The Qur'an is our law. Jihad is our way. Dying in the way of Allah is our highest hope."[18]

Islamist Recep Tayyip Erdogan, Prime Minister of what was once semi-secular Turkey, paraphrased that motto in 1998 in a poem:

"The minarets are our bayonets, the domes our helmets, the mosques our barracks, and the faithful our army."[19.]

The poem earned him a jail sentence and banishment from Turkish politics. However, the Turkish constitution was changed in 2001 and this allowed him to enter politics again.

Al-Banna also warned:

> "It is in the nature of Islam to dominate, not to be dominated, to impose its law on all nations and to extend its power to the entire planet."[20.]

As with Vladimir Lenin and Adolf Hitler, "democracy" is a value to Islam only as a means to an end, which is political and religious supremacy. Once it has been accomplished, "democracy" may be discarded. The Brotherhood's supreme spiritual guide, Muhammed Mahdi Akef, in 2007 observed:

> "The final, absolute message from heaven contains all the values which the secular world claims to have invented....Islam and its values antedated the West by founding true democracy."[21.]

By "true democracy" Akef means a totalitarian, Islamic theocracy. If the term "democracy" means anything, it means majority rule and the majority deciding whether or not you have a right to live or die. If Muslims are in the majority, the rights of non-Muslims are forfeit, and their lives or deaths are determined at the whim or discretion of the collective – the *Ummah* – and its all-powerful voice, the State, or the *Caliphate*.

CAIR and The Brotherhood are closely affiliated with Hamas, which remains designated as a terrorist organization.

Hamas is described by the Federal CounterTerrorism Center:

HAMAS formed in late 1987 at the beginning of the first Palestinian Intifada (uprising). Its roots are in the Palestinian branch of the Muslim Brotherhood, and it is supported by a robust social/political structure inside the Palestinian territories. The group's charter calls for establishing an Islamic Palestinian state in place of Israel and rejects all agreements made between the PLO and Israel....

HAMAS has a paramilitary arm, the Izz al-Din al-Qassam Brigades, which, beginning in the 1990s, has conducted many anti-Israeli attacks in Israel and the Palestinian territories. These have included large-scale terrorist bombings against Israeli civilian targets, as well as small-arms attacks, improvised roadside explosives, and the launching of rockets into Israel.[22]

Hamas is a Sunni terrorist organization (more or less in a "gentleman's" alliance with Sunni Saudi Arabia). While the CounterTerrorism description attempts to paint Hamas as a group working to restrain rocket and terrorist attacks on Israel, nevertheless the fact remains it is a terrorist group controlled by terrorists. It is an outlaw organization and ought to be wiped out.

Hamas has sleeper cells in the U.S., one of which awoke to execute the Boston Marathon bombings of April 15th. According to the Urban Warfare Analysis Center (UWAC):

The most likely future attack by a Hamas or Hezbollah sleeper cell within the next two years would come from a rogue group, barring an aggressive invasion of Iran or Palestine by U.S. forces that operationalize Hamas and Hezbollah groups. Rogue cells often lack the capabilities to launch a sophisticated and synchronized attack, suggesting their actions would be more spontaneous, opportunistic, and smaller in scale.[23]

UWAC describes four kinds of these sleeper cells:

The characteristics of individual groups frame the likely triggers, tactics, and targets used in potential future sleeper cell attacks. An *infiltration cell* describes a foreign trained cell entering the United States, legally or illegally, to perform an attack when ordered by the organization's leadership. A *homegrown cell* is a collection of radicalized Americans that band together to act in the name of Hamas or Hezbollah, likely without consent from or communication with the leadership of either group.

A *hybrid cell* involves a trained infiltrator entering the United States to join forces with homegrown radicals, producing the most lethal combination of outside expertise and local knowledge. An *independent cell* is a rogue group that breaks away from the strategic directive of the main organization; for example, Hezbollah members crossing the Mexican border to plan an attack contrary to the wishes of Hezbollah leaders.

Two trends are acting to intensify the threat of homegrown and hybrid cells, namely prison radicalization and Internet indoctrination. The lack of qualified imams for prison ministry allows unqualified, radical imams to mentor incarcerated criminals and steer them toward a radicalized worldview. Likewise, the Internet provides a forum for individuals to self-radicalize and connect with extremists anywhere in the world.

Dave Gaubatz, a former federal counter intelligence and counter terrorism officer, has written extensively on the presence of Islamic terrorist cells here in the U.S. In his *Family Security Matters* article of January 2011, "Sleeper Cells in the USA," he wrote:

> 1. The terrorist groups such as Hezbollah, Hamas, and Al-Quaeda each had different leaders and to some degree operated in different ways, but they each had the same two goals (destroy Israel and destroy America and any country that supported either.)…

2. Terrorist sleeper cells are located primarily in Virginia, New York, North Carolina, Michigan, Florida, California, and Canada. The "sleepers" are prepared to conduct terrorist attacks within the U.S., and nuclear material is available to them. "Prepared" in this instance indicates they have the necessary tools to carry out their attacks and are prepared to die....

Terrorist operations are active in the U.S. and are being operated/financed by Al-Qaeda throughout the U.S.[24]

The Investigative Project on Terrorism has completed a map of known terrorist cells that have been established in the U.S. as of 2007.[25]

Gaubatz participated in the *Mapping Sharia Project*, which sought to identify what percentage of the approximately 2,300 mosques in the U.S. advocated violent and terrorist *jihad* to their congregations. Here are some of its findings, correlated and published by Mordechai Kedar and David Yerushalmi:

A random survey of 100 representative mosques in the U.S. was conducted to measure the correlation between Sharia adherence and dogma calling for violence against non-believers. Of the 100 mosques surveyed, 51% had texts on site rated as severely advocating violence; 30% had texts rated as moderately advocating violence; and 19% had no violent texts at all. Mosques that presented as Sharia adherent were more likely to feature violence-positive texts on site than were their non-Sharia-adherent counterparts.

In 84.5% of the mosques, the imam recommended studying violence-positive texts. The leadership at Sharia-adherent mosques was more likely to recommend that a worshiper study violence-positive texts than leadership at non-Sharia-adherent mosques. Fifty-eight percent of the mosques invited guest imams known to promote violent jihad. The leadership of mosques that featured violence-positive literature was more likely to invite guest imams who were known to promote violent jihad than was the leadership cf mosques that did not feature violence-positive literature on mosque premises.[26]

The next major terrorist group, Al Qada, or Al-Qa'ida, a Sunni terrorist organization, is also described by the CounterTerrorism site:

> Established by Osama Bin Ladin in 1988 with Arabs who fought in Afghanistan against the Soviet Union, al-Qaʻida's declared goal is the establishment of a pan-Islamic caliphate throughout the Muslim world. Toward this end, al-Qaʻida seeks to unite Muslims to fight the West, especially the United States, as a means of overthrowing Muslim regimes al-Qaʻida deems "apostate," expelling Western influence from Muslim countries, and defeating Israel. Al-Qaʻida issued a statement in February 1998 under the banner of "the World Islamic Front for Jihad Against the Jews and Crusaders" saying it was the duty of all Muslims to kill US citizens—civilian and military—and their allies everywhere. The group merged with the Egyptian Islamic Jihad (al-Jihad) in June 2001.
>
> On 11 September 2001, 19 al-Qaʻida suicide attackers hijacked and crashed four US commercial jets—two into the World Trade Center in New York City, one into the Pentagon near Washington, D.C., and a fourth into a field in Shanksville, Pennsylvania— leaving nearly 3,000 people dead. Al-Qaʻida also directed the 12 October 2000 attack on the USS Cole in the port of Aden, Yemen, which killed 17 US sailors and injured another 39, and conducted the bombings in August 1998 of the US embassies in Nairobi, Kenya, and Dar es Salaam, Tanzania, killing 224 people and injuring more than 5,000. Since 2002, al-Qaʻida and affiliated groups have conducted attacks worldwide, including in Europe, North Africa, South Asia, Southeast Asia, and the Middle East.[27]

Hezbollah, or Hizballah, is another major terrorist gang allied with the Iranian government, which is ruled by the Shi'ite or Shia sect of Islam. CounterTerrorism describes Hezbollah:

Formed in 1982 in response to the Israeli invasion of Lebanon, Hizballah (the "Party of God"), a Lebanon-based Shia terrorist group, advocates Shia empowerment within Lebanon. The group also supports Palestinian rejectionist groups in their struggle against Israel and provides training for Iraqi Shia militants attacking Coalition forces in Iraq. A Hizballah operative, Ali Musa Daqduq, faces US military charges of coming to Iraq to train extremists, and of being responsible for an attack against a military facility in Karbala', Iraq, in January 2007 that left five American soldiers dead.

Hizballah has been involved in numerous anti-US terrorist attacks, including the suicide truck bombings of the US Embassy in Beirut in April 1983, the US Marine barracks in Beirut in October 1983, and the US Embassy annex in Beirut in September 1984, as well as the hijacking of TWA 847 in 1985 and the Khobar Towers attack in Saudi Arabia in 1996. Although Hizballah's leadership is based in Lebanon, the group has established cells worldwide.[28]

There are other active, Islamic terrorist gangs around the world: Boko Haram in Nigeria, which has declared war on Christians in that country, killing hundreds, if not thousands; Al-Shabaab in Somalia; The Imarat Kavkaz, (IK, or Caucasus Emirate), founded in late 2007 by Chechen extremist Doku Umarov, is an Islamist militant organization based in Russia's North Caucasus, whose stated goal is the liberation of what it considers to be Muslim lands from Moscow; and the Abu Sayyaf Group of terrorists in the Philippines.

Finally, there is the Taliban ("student army" of Islam) in Pakistan and Afghanistan.

Tehrik-e Taliban Pakistan (TTP) is an alliance of militant groups in Pakistan formed in 2007 to unify groups fighting against the Pakistani military in the Federally Administered Tribal Areas and Khyber Pakhtunkhwa. TTP leaders also hope to impose a strict interpretation of Qur'anic instruction throughout Pakistan and to expel Coalition troops from Afghanistan. TTP maintains close ties to senior al-Qa'ida

leaders, including al-Qa'ida's former head of operations in Pakistan.

Baitullah Mahsud, the first TTP leader, was killed in an explosion on 5 August 2009 and was succeeded by Hakimullah Mahsud, who vowed to deploy suicide operatives to the United States. The group has repeatedly threatened to attack the US homeland, and a TTP spokesman claimed responsibility for the failed vehicle bomb attack in Times Square in New York City on 1 May 2010. In June 2011, a spokesman vowed to attack the United States and Europe in revenge for the death of Osama Bin Ladin.[29]

One of the most wasteful, fruitless, and costly in terms of American lives and treasure, has been the American military campaign waged in Afghanistan and Pakistan for the last ten years. Aside from propping up the corrupt and often anti-American Karzai régime in Afghanistan at the cost of billions of dollars, the U.S. and its allies have been stabbed in the back by Pakistan's government numerous times such as when it allowed Pakistan to serve as a refuge for Taliban and Al Qada forces.[30]

Osama bin Laden, author of 9/11, on the run for twelve years, was hiding in a private compound near a village, Abbottabad, Pakistan, presumably with the knowledge and permission of the Pakistani government. A U.S. Navy SEAL team raided the compound in May 2012, killing bin Laden.[31]

World News Daily (WND) has published a credible report that Iran was the chief instigator of the Boston Marathon bombings.

Qasem Soleimani, the head of Iran's Quds Forces, ordered reconnaissance and intelligence gathering on various events and public gatherings in the United States years ago, culminating in the bombings at the Boston Marathon one week ago, WND has learned.

> According to a source within Iran's intelligence services, the Islamic regime's Quds Forces, a special unit of the Revolutionary Guards in charge of extraterritorial operations, have done extensive planning on gatherings, events and high-value targets in the United States for some time, but for two years focused on events such as the Boston Marathon.[32]

Iran, however, apparently had help.

> The source had earlier provided information that tied the Islamic regime to the Boston attack and pointed to the collaboration of the regime's Quds Forces with the Lebanese terrorist group Hezbollah and elements of al-Qaida with links to an operational center in South Asia. He said that under Quds Force guidance, Hezbollah recruited sympathizers through collaborators connected to South Asia for terrorist activities in the U.S.[33]

This kind of cooperation underscores the fact that even though these terrorist groups have maintained mutual, decades-old enmities towards each other, and are in seeming competition to see who can murder and destroy the most. In many instances they are all prepared to cooperate to bring down the "Great Satan," the United States, and to obliterate the "Little Satan," Israel.

> Their goal... is to divert attention to Saudi Arabia and other Sunni countries that are in a proxy war with Iran over leadership in the region. As Iran is trying to destabilize Bahrain, Yemen and Saudi Arabia itself, those countries are trying to destabilize Syria, where Saudi Arabia and other Sunni states hope to oust Assad and confront Hezbollah.

> Iran is prepared to continue such attacks within the U.S. homeland to create fear and uncertainty and divert America's

push to stop Iran's nuclear program and oust Assad, he said. In that regard, Iran extended its recruitment operations to the Caucasus, Dagestan and Chechnya, a move that Russia has

denounced. Iran also has a major operational center in Azerbaijan, where tensions between that government and the Islamic regime remain high. Many terrorists have been arrested within Azerbaijan.

...The two brothers who set off the bombs at the Boston Marathon were assets of a bigger network and were set up to be burned so there would be no link back to their handlers – and Iran. The source added that in the view of the Islamic regime, the terrorist attack in Boston was a success because U.S. homeland security was breached, much fear was created, and international media spread details of the attack — all with no direct link to the regime itself.[34]

The Tsarnaev killers attended one of the most "radical," i.e., ideologically consistent, mosques the Boston area. They are sister mosques, the Islamic Society of Boston Cultural Center (Boston) and the Islamic Society of Boston (Cambridge). However, these mosques, like dozens throughout the U.S., are closely linked to the Islamic Society of North America (ISNA), which in turn is a front for the Muslim Brotherhood.

Other Muslim organizations in the U.S., such as CAIR, the Islamic Circle of North America (ICNA), the Islamic Society of North America (ISNA), the Muslim Public Affairs Council (MPAC), and the Muslim American Society (MAS). The Muslim Student Association (MSA) is the oldest Muslim organization in the country, founded in 1963. These are all Brotherhood fronts or have close ties to the Brotherhood. Each of these entities has chapters in virtually every state of the union and in major cities, and with sister chapters in Canada.

The Muslim American Society is noted for promoting conflict with the United States, causing ethnic or nationalist Muslims to feel nostalgic for their home countries, and to seek comfort in the global Islamist political community rather than in America.[35.]

Daniel Greenfield, in a *FrontPage* article of April 24, "Russia Repeatedly Warned U.S. About Muslim Boston Bomber," underscores the anemic efforts of the FBI and intelligence agencies to spot *jihadist* trouble in the making and to "connect the dots":

> You can't connect the dots if you can't address motive. Without Islam as the motive, there was no reason to believe that Tamerlan Tsarnaev was a threat to anyone but Russia. The FBI, under the influence of political correctness, likely chose to see him as a Chechen nationalist. But a Chechen nationalist is generally a Muslim terrorist. And Muslim terrorists don't limit their sphere of terror to just one country.[36.]

Oren Dorell in *USA Today* noted that the Cambridge mosque also denied responsibility or knowledge for the Tsarnaev brothers' "radicalization."

> A statement issued by the Cambridge mosque said the Tsarnaev brothers were "occasional visitors." The mosque's office manager, Nichole Mossalam, said neither brother expressed radical views. "They never exhibited any violent sentiments or behaviors. Otherwise, they would have been reported," Mossalam said.[37.]

However, as in countless other instances, what Islamic spokesmen say in public differs dramatically from what they think or say privately to their colleagues or the "Arab street." Islam sanctions the common and deceptive practice of *taqiyya*, or Islamic double-speak, of deceiving or lying to the infidel or enemy.

For example, *The New York Post*, in an article by Mitchell Bard on August 22, 2010, "On mosque, beware the Saudis," cites once instance of *taqiyya* employed in a mosque itself:

In 2003, US Ambassador to Saudi Arabia Robert Jordan said, "We have noticed lately in influential mosques the imam has condemned terrorism and preached in favor of tolerance, then closed the sermon with 'Oh God, please destroy the Jews, the infidels, and all who support them.'"[38.]

In addition from the Tsarnaev brothers, other Muslims who preach violent *jihadist* terrorism have passed through the doors of both mosques. According to Dorell in *USA Today*:

> • Alamoudi, who signed the articles of incorporation as the Cambridge mosque's president, was sentenced to 23 years in federal court in Alexandria, Va., in 2004 for his role as a facilitator in what federal prosecutors called a Libyan assassination plot against then-crown prince Abdullah of Saudi Arabia. Abdullah is now the Saudi king.

> • Aafia Siddiqui, who occasionally prayed at the Cambridge mosque, was arrested in Afghanistan in 2008 while in possession of cyanide canisters and plans for a chemical attack in New York City. She tried to grab a rifle while in detention and shoot at military officers and FBI agents, for which she was convicted in New York in 2010 and is serving an 86-year sentence.

> • Tarek Mehanna, who worshiped at the Cambridge mosque, was sentenced in 2012 to 17 years in prison for conspiring to aid al-Qaeda. Mehanna had traveled to Yemen to seek terrorist training and plotted to use automatic weapons to shoot up a mall in the Boston suburbs, federal investigators in Boston alleged.

> • Ahmad Abousamra, the son of a former vice president of the Muslim American Society Boston Abdul-Badi Abousamra, was identified by the FBI as Mehanna's co-conspirator. He fled to Syria and is wanted by the FBI on charges of providing support

to terrorists and conspiracy to kill Americans in a foreign country.

• Jamal Badawi of Canada, a former trustee of the Islamic Society of Boston Trust, which owns both mosques, was named as a non-indicted co-conspirator in the 2007 Holy Land Foundation terrorism trial in Texas over the funneling of money to Hamas, which is the Palestinian wing of the Muslim Brotherhood.[39.]

Dorell emphasizes the link between the Boston/Cambridge mosques and the Muslim American Society.

What both mosques have in common is an affiliation with the Muslim American Society, an organization founded in 1993 that describes itself as an American Islamic revival movement. It has also been described by federal prosecutors in court as the "overt arm" of the Muslim Brotherhood, which calls for Islamic law and is the parent organization of Hamas, a U.S.-designated terrorist group.[40.]

Freedom House's Center for Religious Freedom published in 2005 a 90-page study of how Saudi Wahhabist "hate" literature is used in countless American mosques to promote *jihad* and dissatisfaction with the U.S. and with American culture. The study compared literature found in America mosques with literature and textbooks used by the Saudi Arabian government, in Saudi schools and other Saudi institutions, and covers all facets of Muslim/unbeliever relationships, from friendships to business to social niceties.

The study states:

To be sure, not all the books in such mosques espouse extremism and not all extremist works are Saudi. Saudi Arabia, however, is overwhelmingly the state most responsible for the publications on the ideology of hate in America.

The Center for Religious Freedom has gathered samples of over 200 such texts over the last twelve months -- all from American mosques and all spread, sponsored or otherwise generated by

Saudi Arabia. They demonstrate the ongoing indoctrination of Muslims in the United States in the hostility and belligerence of Saudi Arabia's hardliner *Wahhabi* sect of Islam.[41]

For example, page 27 of the study begins:

> Cordial relations with Christians, Jews and other non-Muslims must have the sole purpose of leading them to Islam. The Wahhabis prohibit friendships with infidels exceeding those with other Muslims, or giving these infidels preference in employment and the like. On the other hand, accepting invitations to Christian homes and sharing meals with them is acceptable for certain purposes and provided one is sure that the Islamic dietary laws are kept. The Saudi government *fatwa* publication [Document No. 52] that was collected from an American mosque gives instruction on interactions with Christians, Jews, and other infidels in the West where Muslims live in minority communities. Can we enter their homes? Yes, in order to advise them and point out the right path to them, not with the intention of friendship or loyalty. Similarly, infidels can visit Muslims in their homes as long as the women of the household are covered and segregated, and only in order to preach Islam to them [Document No. 52].[42]

The study further notes that "Wahhabi teachings . . . are murderously intolerant toward the Shi'a, Jews, Baha'i, Ahmadiyya, homosexuals, apostates and 'unbelievers' of all kinds, and horribly repressive with respect to everyone else, especially women . . . These are essentially the same basic beliefs as those expressed by al Qaeda."[43]

ISLAM IS A RELIGION OF TERROR

Commonly, the noun *Islam* is qualified by most commentators with the suffix "ism" or "ist," or referred to as "militant" or "radical" Islam. Terrorists are usually referred to as Islamic "extremists," "radicals," or "militants." This practice suggests that Islam is an ideology which is not inherently malevolent, belligerent, or hell-bent on conquest. If it were not for the "crazed" hijackers and suicide bombers, such qualified usage implies, Islam would be just another topic of conversation at cocktail parties.

Bosch Fawstin explains the fatal fallacy of radicalizing individual terrorists, while giving the ideology a pass:

> Western intellectuals and commentators refer to the enemy's ideology as: "Islamic Fundamentalism," "Islamic Extremism," "Totalitarian Islam," "Islamofascism," "Political Islam," "Militant Islam," "Bin Ladenism," "Islamonazism," "Radical Islam," "Islamism," etc....
>
> The enemy calls it "Islam."
>
> Imagine, if during past wars, we used terms such as "Radical Nazism," "Extremist Shinto" and "Militant Communism." The implication would be that there are good versions of those ideologies, which would then lead some to seek out "moderate" Nazis. Those who use terms other than "Islam" create the impression that it's some variant of Islam that's behind the enemy that we're facing. A term such as "Militant Islam" is redundant, but our politicians continue praising Islam as if it were their own religion. Bush told us "Islam is peace" — after 2,996 Americans were murdered in its name. He maintained that illusion throughout his two terms, and never allowed our soldiers to defeat the enemy.[44]

On complaints by CAIR that FBI and Army counter-intelligence training materials "denigrated" or "defamed" Islam, those materials were subsequently discarded or revised.[47] If the FBI is regarded as a kind of half-blind Mr. Magoo, stumbling around attempting to identify

Islamic terrorists and terrorist plots without the necessary, legal right to identify them, then the country is left that much defenseless against Islamic terrorist attacks. Tamerlan Tsarnaev, the Boston bomber, was in the "system," but because he had been interviewed once, he was not allowed to be interviewed again.

President Barack Obama, in both of his terms of office since 2009, has not only followed in George W. Bush's footsteps in that regard, calling Islam a "religion of peace," but has "reached out" to Muslims and Islam far more than had Bush and in too many ways to recount here. Let us just note that Muslims associated with the Muslim Brotherhood now hold key positions in our intelligence community, in the State Department, and can be found in the military. Prominent Muslims often act as "experts" or consultants to advise various government agencies on how to present Islam in the best light and how to avoid "stereotyping" Muslims and Islam.[45]

THE CULTURAL ROOTS OF TERRORISM

The cancerous progress of Islam in the West is made possible by, among other modern "isms," multiculturalism and egalitarianism.

Egalitarianism seeks "equality of results." Outcomes and results must be equal for all, whether the value is wealth, fame, honors, or admission to prestigious colleges. In pushing redistribution schemes, egalitarians regard as irrelevant one's talent, intelligence, effort, virtue. To rectify the so-called unfairness of some individuals being more talented or more able than others, egalitarians tell us that we must hobble, raze, and ridicule the best. We must "comfort the afflicted, and afflict the comfortable." We must give our heroes feet of clay. We must sacrifice the best to the worst.

In practice, egalitarianism means that a criminal empire is to be admired as much as Steve Jobs' computer empire, that we must have scoreless soccer games to bolster the feelings of less talented players, that beauty contests "disadvantage" the ugly, that the healthy make the obese feel bad.

Egalitarianism demands non-judgmental acceptance of everyone's opinions. (There is no absolute truth, the purveyors of egalitarianism say, and no knowable reality in which to find it.) Since no opinion or value judgment is more valid than any another, egalitarianism reduces all such judgments to the lowest common denominator. On this view, Aristotle's gift of reason to Western civilization, the Renaissance his philosophy spawned, and the science-loving Enlightenment that improved man's life – all of this is to be immolated to the death-worshipping creed of Islam.

Multiculturalism is egalitarianism applied to cultures. It proclaims that no culture is superior to another. In practice, the only way to achieve such equality of results among cultures is to tear down the best, i.e., the West. To achieve equality between the great and the depraved, we must, claim multiculturalists, surrender to Islamic terror and tyranny our freedoms and wealth. After all, say multiculturalists, who are we to claim that it's better to use an airplane for travel than it is to use one for mass murder?

The disease of multiculturalism spreads like this. First it blurs all cultural distinctions, i.e., it performs a kind of value lobotomy on the minds in the West. Then any second-rate, third-rate, or nihilistic cultural "values" rush in to fill the void. One sees examples of this in the demands that the Ground Zero mosque be afforded the same respect as the Iwo Jima monument in Washington D.C., or in the calls for the use of Sharia law instead of Western jurisprudence.

The Western mind used to value Patrick Henry's "give me liberty or give me death," the *Bill of Rights*, and the *Declaration of Independence*. But those "cultural prejudices" are being wiped clean by multiculturalism. And now, the West's values are being sacrificed to the lowest and worst culture on earth – an Islamic culture that today demands submission to its reign of terror.

But, philosophically and morally, Islam is an ideology of *nihilism*.

What is nihilism? Briefly, according to *The Merriam-Webster Dictionary*, its philosophical meaning is "a doctrine that denies any objective ground of truth and especially of moral truths." Its political meaning is "a doctrine or belief that conditions in the social organization are so bad as to make destruction desirable for its own sake *independent of any constructive program or possibility*." (*Italics mine*) This means that values as such are candidates for destruction for destruction's sake.[46.]

In Islam, no values may be held outside its prescribed values, and *all* its values are anti-reason, inherently irrational, anti-man, and, fundamentally anti-life. Islamic "values" purportedly are handed down to men by a deity who commands obedience; "Do as I say, because I say so." All other values, *including* one's life, are of no consequence and may be eliminated or destroyed *because* they are non-Islamic and conflict with the whole psychology and ideology of submission to the arbitrary diktats of an unknowable being. Islam, in essence, is a creed of living death.

While Islam's brand of nihilism predates by millennia the formulation of the concept of nihilism, one philosopher in particular is responsible for its spread in the West and for the concomitant acceptance in the West of Islam as just another benign religion to which violent "extremists" have given a "bad name." That philosopher is Immanuel Kant. The term *nihilism*, however, was coined by his 18th century contemporary, German Idealist Friedrich Heinrich Jacobi, who, in his own revolt against the Enlightenment, denied the possibility of objective grounds of knowledge, and claimed that "truth" can only be known through *feeling* and *faith*. Like Kant, he devised a system of "reason" in the name of "revelation" by denying the validity of reason.

Kant's philosophical system is much more elaborate and better known. His major works are efforts to defend religion from Enlightenment ideas and influences. To achieve that, he claimed that reality is unknowable, and that reason is the barrier to ultimate truth.[47.]

Kant's system of ethics paves the way for Islam's moral code. Central to his ethics is the notion that one has a duty, an unchosen obligation, to sacrifice one's personal inclinations and desires. If one is motivated by personal gain, then one gets no moral credit. The desire for happiness here on earth, claims Kant, is the most evil of all. On this view, the purpose of life is self-abnegation, pain, and suffering. The destruction of values *because* they are values is the essence of nihilism. And in theory and practice, that is Islam.

The next time you read about Islamic suicide bombers and attacks on Americans or Westerners here or abroad, or watch on TV mobs of maniacal Muslims shouting death to America and to hell with freedom of speech, you are witnessing not so much Muslims obeying Mohammad's commands, as seeing Kant's philosophically selfless progeny at work.

To destroy man's desire for happiness and values, one must first destroy reason. Gary Hull, publisher of Voltaire Press, raised an important issue about how Islam is impervious to reason.

> "One philosophic key to why, by its nature, Islam is more violent today, and even fascist, than are Christianity and Judaism, is that Islam was never defanged by the Renaissance or the Enlightenment. It was never dragged, kicking and screaming, in acknowledgement of the key political idea of the separation of religion and state. When Ethan Allen, who, like many of the Founders, was a Deist, penned his pamphlet, *Reason: The Only Oracle of Man*, that idea never reached the Islamic world."[48]

And if, perchance, some sultan, caliph, imam or mullah had heard of the idea, it must have been promptly rejected. Reason is antithetical to religious and secular tyrants.

Further, Islam is *anti-intellectual*. Its key documents, the *Koran*, the *Hadith*, and the *Sira*, must be learned by rote memorization. There is no system in them, no underlying logic to their contents. By comparison, much of Christianity and Judaism (because of the influences of ancient Greece and, later, the Renaissance) use elements of Aristotelian logic to reach their conclusions, and to proselytize for their ideologies. But most of the statements in the *Koran* are mere assertions reputedly uttered by Mohammad; in the *Hadith* and *Sira*, instructional anecdotes and homilies of his and his cohorts' barbarity. There are no moral principles that govern Islam, other than to resort to force against men who resist conversion to it or submission as serfs, slaves, or *dhimmis*.

"Moderate" Muslims protest that the *Koran* can be read so that benign moral tenets can be construed and abided by. But because the *Koran* is a permanent declaration of war against man's happiness and reason, there is no way any of its belligerent statements can be "interpreted" to mean anything other than what they say.[49] For example:

Koran 9:5 – Fight and kill the disbelievers wherever you find them, take them captive, harass them, lie in wait and ambush them using every stratagem of war.

Koran 9:112 – The Believers fight in Allah's Cause, they slay and are slain, kill and are killed.

Koran 9:29 – Fight those who do not believe until they all surrender, paying the protective tax [*jizya*] in submission.

Koran 8:39 – So fight them until there is no more *Fitna* and all submit to the religion of Allah alone (in the whole world).

Muhammad ibn Ishāq ibn Yasār ibn Khiyār was an 8th century Muslim hagiographer and historian, one of many such collectors of the oral traditions of Islam for the *Sira*. Here are a handful of his "interpretations" of Islam:

Ishāq 324 – "He said, 'Fight them so that there is no more rebellion, and religion, all of it, is for Allah only. Allah must have no rivals.'"

Ishāq 440 – "Helped by the Holy Spirit we smote Muhammad's foes. The Apostle sent a message to them with a sharp cutting sword."

Ishāq 470 – "We attacked them fully armed, swords in hand, cutting through heads and skulls."

"Moderate" Muslims cannot rationally defend Islam. Islam can only be repudiated, root, branch, and tree. Only reason and a this-worldly philosophy can attempt accomplish that goal. And should all the belligerent and anecdotal imperatives be excised from the *Koran* and its companion texts, what would be left would no longer be Islam. There is no more reconciliation possible between reason and the nihilism of Islam than there is between the Bill of Rights and the Mafia code of *Il bacio della morte* ("Kiss of death" bestowed upon a gang's traitor). Islam is incompatible with reason and with life itself.

STATES THAT SPONSOR TERRORISM

The State Department's National Center for Counter Terrorism lists forty-eight terrorist groups, the majority of them Islamic.[50] But the State Department itself currently lists only four state sponsors of terrorism: Cuba, the Sudan, Iran and Syria.[51] Libya was dropped from the list after the downfall of Omar Qadhaffi, but should be reinstated, for it is now being governed by Muslim Brotherhood and Al Qada proxies. Missing from the State Department list are Saudi Arabia, Pakistan, and Qatar. Egypt, now under the thumb of the Muslim Brotherhood, may in the future qualify as a state that sponsors terrorism.

Other Islamic states that have supported terrorism in the way of transitional locales with the knowledge or support of their governments are Yemen and Somalia. Iraq, "freed" by us from the grip of Saddam Hussein with American lives and treasure, has become a client state of Iran. Indonesia has the highest population of Muslims and also acts as a covert go-between for the funding and coordination of terrorist plots between competing terrorist groups.

Islam as an ideological force is stateless. But states sponsor its actions. Iran is the chief instigator and enabler of Islamic terrorism.

John David Lewis, in his seminal study of warfare, *Nothing Less Than Victory: Decisive Wars and the Lessons of History*, writes that warfare requires of its civilian and military leaders the proper philosophy to defeat an enemy, a philosophy which must include a moral reason. He demonstrates the efficacy of this philosophy by describing the conduct of several wars from the past, from the Greco-Persian Wars between 547 and 446 BC to the American victory over Japan in 1945.

The United States professes to be "at war against terrorism." Yet, while Islamic terrorism is a fact, our government refuses to acknowledge that it is Islam that has declared war against the West. Islam is a "religion of peace," it repeats over and over again; it is only against its "militants," "radicals," and "extremists" that we must take action against. Islam is not totalitarian, it is merely another religion whose adherents must not be offended or provoked. We have only to fear its foot soldiers, the terrorists. Once we have captured, neutralized, or killed them, we can live in peace.

But Islam has an inexhaustible pool of Muslims willing to die as "martyrs." Western leaders and intellectuals refuse to consider the source: Islam itself. So the "war on terror" will continue indefinitely, wasting lives, treasure, and time, until the U.S. is ground down by an enemy dedicated to conquest and victory.

Lewis wrote in his Introduction, "Victory and the Moral Will to Fight":

> Americans today have been told to expect years of military action overseas. Yet they are also being told that they should not expect victory; that a "definitive end to the conflict" is not possible; and that success will mean a level of violence that "does not define our daily lives." A new administration [Obama] is now bringing more troops into Afghanistan – where American troops have been operating for eight years – but without defining the terms of victory. The change in American

military doctrine behind these developments occurred with astonishing speed; in 1939 American military planners still chose their objectives on the basis of the following understanding: "Decisive defeat in battle breaks the enemy's will to war and forces him to sue for peace which is the national aim."[52]

"Victory," notes Lewis, has become a moral anathema to modern military planners and civilian policymakers.

The change in doctrine is not due primarily to the horrific destructiveness of modern war, for American leaders have adopted such aims even for conflicts that do not threaten to "go nuclear." We inhabit a moral climate in which any attempt by victors to impose cultural values onto others is roundly condemned. We have largely accepted that the pursuit of victory would necessarily create new grievances and guarantee an even more destructive conflict in the future. This is a moral issue.

But this idea should be questioned.[53]

Islam, a State-enforced ideology that has declared war on the West, is seeking to break the will of the West to resist by exploiting our own egalitarian and altruist policies. Western values of freedom and individual rights, declare instructors at West Point and other service academies, in war colleges, and at the Pentagon, should not be imposed on the adherents of Islam. To impose them would be to commit the "sin" of "cultural imperialism."

We now have had a succession of Commanders-in-Chief and an emasculated military dedicated to defending this country against its enemies by adopting a policy of not identifying either the enemy or a rational reason for fighting him.

Lewis, expanding on Carl von Clausewitz's famous treatise, *On War*, emphasizes that:

> A commander's most urgent task is to identify this central point for his enemy's overall war effort and to direct his forces to that center – be it economic, social, or military – with a view to collapsing the opponent's commitment to continue the war. to break the "will to fight" is to reverse not only the political decision to continue the war by inducing a decision to

> surrender, but also the commitment of the population to continue (or restart) the war.

> To force this reversal of the decision and commitment to fight, a commander must *know himself, his own people, his enemy, and his enemy's people – and, he must know his own moral objective as well as that of his enemy.*[54] (*Italics* original)

With few exceptions, our politicians and mainstream intellectuals do not grasp the essence of Islam, and do not have the moral rectitude to defend America. Our enemy, however, does know, and does have a blood-thirsty desire to achieve its goals – which is world-wide poverty, slavery, and destruction. To quote from the Brotherhood's 1991 *Explanatory Memorandum: A General Strategic Goal for the Group in North America*:

> The process of settlement is a "Civilization-Jihadist Process" with all the word means. The Ikhwan [the Brothers] must understand that their work in America is a kind of grand Jihad in eliminating and destroying the Western civilization from within and "sabotaging" its miserable house by their hands and the hands of the believers so that it is eliminated and God's religion is made victorious over all other religions.[55]

Our country is indeed self-destructing in the "miserable" hands of its quavering, irrational, evasive, and morally rudderless policymakers. In contrast, Islam has never been afraid of using the term "victory," and hasn't the least inhibition in imposing its "cultural values" on the rest of the world.

The West, and especially the U.S., has demonstrated time and again that it hasn't the will to resist.

Dr. Leonard Peikoff, the preeminent Ayn Rand scholar alive today, wrote shortly after the 9/11 attacks, "End States Who Sponsor Terrorism." The essay appeared in a full-page ad in *The New York Times* on October 2nd, 2001.[56.] Such an ad would never be accepted by the *Times* today.

> The Muslim countries embodied in an extreme form every idea – selfless duty, anti-materialism, faith or feeling above science, the supremacy of the group – which our universities, our churches, and our own political Establishment had long been upholding as virtue. When two groups, our leadership and theirs, accept the same basic ideas, the most consistent side wins.

Islam has been nothing but consistent, from its very beginnings in the 7th century up through the 21st. The West, and especially the U.S., to avoid being called "extremist" or "Islamophobic," has consistently responded with a patchwork of pragmatic policies that eschew any kind of consistent, principled stand against a committed enemy, policies which evade identifying the enemy and which have surrendered ground to the terrorists and their sponsors on virtually every occasion. And on every occasion, such policies have backfired – as in Afghanistan, Egypt and Libya – and only emboldened Islamic terrorists and their sponsors.

One weblog's motto is, "It isn't Islamophobia if they really are trying to kill you." Our political leadership refuses to believe that Islam is a killer ideology, even as piles of bodies grow at their feet.

Many nations work to fill our body bags. But Iran, according to a State Department report of 1999, is "the most active state sponsor of terrorism," training and arming groups from all over the Mideast, including Islamic Jihad, Hamas, and Hezbollah. Nor is Iran's government now "moderating." Five months ago, the world's leading terrorist groups resolved to unite in a holy war against the U.S., which they called "a second Israel"; their meeting was held in Teheran. (*Fox News*, 9/16/01)

Peikoff writes about the purblind military strategy of pursuing and eradicating the foot soldiers of Islam, the terrorists, but not the states that sponsor them.

For over a decade, there was another guarantee of American impotence: the notion that a terrorist is alone responsible for his actions, and that each, therefore, must be tried as an individual before a court of law. This viewpoint, thankfully, is fading; most people now understand that terrorists exist only through the sanction and support of a government.

We need not prove the identity of any of these creatures, because terrorism is not an issue of personalities. It cannot be stopped by destroying bin Laden and the al-Qaeda army, or even by destroying the destroyers everywhere. If that is all we do, a new army of militants will soon rise up to replace the old one.

The behavior of such militants is that of the regimes which make them possible. Their atrocities are not crimes, but acts of war. The proper response, as the public now understands, is a war in self-defense. In the excellent words of Paul Wolfowitz, deputy secretary of defense, we must "end states who sponsor terrorism."

What have we now as a Secretary of State, a Secretary of Defense, and a Director of the Central Intelligence Agency (John Brennan, who has reputedly converted to Islam[57])? Three men who dare not breathe a

47

critical word against the enemy, Islam. And as a President, a man who would rather embrace a totalitarian ideology as a force to ensure "world peace"? But the world has been at anything but "peace" for over half a century. The murderous behavior of Islamic terrorists is an accurate and undeniable reflection on the wishes and ends of their state supporters.

When the exponents of Islam say it is a "religion of peace," they mean the peace of victory over the whole world, when there will be no more enemies to conquer, enslave, or destroy. They mean the peace of a cemetery. They mean the peace of zombies, of the living dead.

Peikoff expresses the proper war-fighting philosophy explicated by John Lewis in *Nothing Less Than Victory*, and as long ago as 2001 forecast the irrationality of "Just War Theory" that is being taught in our service academies, and the "Rules of Engagement" under which American soldiers have had to fight our enemies in Iraq and Afghanistan, both policies designed to avoid "collateral" casualties among civilians and to justify retaliatory force.

> A proper war in self-defense is one fought without self-crippling restrictions placed on our commanders in the field. It must be fought with the most effective weapons we possess (a few weeks ago, Rumsfeld refused, correctly, to rule out nuclear weapons). And it must be fought in a manner that secures victory as quickly as possible and with the fewest U.S. casualties, regardless of the countless innocents caught in the line of fire. These innocents suffer and die because of the action of their own government in sponsoring the initiation of force against America. Their fate, therefore, is their government's moral responsibility. There is no way for our bullets to be aimed only at evil men.

Comparing Islam with the Nazis, and Iran with Nazi Germany, Peikoff notes:

> Most of the Mideast is ruled by thugs who would be paralyzed by an American victory over any of their neighbors. Iran, by

contrast, is the only major country there ruled by zealots dedicated not to material gain (such as more wealth or territory), but to the triumph by any means, however violent, of the Muslim fundamentalist movement they brought to life. That is why Iran manufactures the most terrorists.

If one were under a Nazi aerial bombardment, it would be senseless to restrict oneself to combating Nazi satellites while ignoring Germany and the ideological plague it was working to spread. What Germany was to Nazism in the 1940s, Iran is to terrorism today. Whatever else it does, therefore, the U.S. can put an end to the Jihad-mongers only by taking out Iran.

A resistance movement exists in Iran that opposes the regime and its theocratic thugs, the mullahs. But the U.S. has ignored that movement and refused to acknowledge the brutality of the Iranian régime. Instead, it endorses toothless economic sanctions and allows the régime to develop nuclear weapons.

If one wandered into any random university classroom, or read any random editorial or op-ed, one would encounter teachers and writers saying that the U.S. brought 9/11 and the Boston Marathon bombing upon itself, because it neglected the feelings of Muslims and Islamic terrorists. They have accepted the Islamic charge of "blasphemy." It is as true now as it was in 2001.

The greatest obstacle to U.S. victory is not Iran and its allies, but our own intellectuals. Even now, they are advocating the same ideas that caused our historical paralysis. They are asking a reeling nation to show neighbor-love by shunning "vengeance." The multiculturalists – rejecting the concept of objectivity – are urging us to "understand" the Arabs and avoid "racism" (i.e., any condemnation of any group's culture). The friends of "peace" are reminding us, ever more loudly, to "remember Hiroshima" and beware the sin of pride.

These are the kinds of voices being heard in the universities, the churches, and the media as the country recovers from its first shock, and the professoriate et al. feel emboldened to resume business as usual. These voices are a siren song luring us to untroubled sleep while the fanatics proceed to gut America.

What should the U.S. do? The longer we wait, the worse will become the crisis. The disasters of the past, such was World War II, were the result of policies of appeasement and of not wanting to hurt the *feelings* of our enemies. The rationale was that Hitler and Stalin had their own polylogistic views of reality and morality, and who were we to question them? Who were we to uphold our rationality as the sole means of living? We paid the price for that Kantian worldview with a costly world war. We are still paying it, even though Nazi Germany and the Soviet Union are gone. We have a new malignant ideology to face, Islam. And we have had a succession of Presidents who refused to acknowledge it.

Today, we have a President whose actions and words indicate that he understands and approves of that ideology. Our Commander-in-Chief is a demonstrable *nihilist*.

Is it too late to act? Emphatically – no. As the moral heirs of the Founders, we owe it to them and to ourselves to acknowledge our enemy and the moral code that makes him possible. We should never apologize for our ability to end states that sponsor terrorism and work to destroy us and all the fruits of our civilization, nor hesitate to use that power. We should demand of our leaders that they act to secure an American's right to life, liberty, and the pursuit of happiness on earth.

What are the alternatives? We either end states that sponsor terrorism, or they will end us. Those are the only alternatives. It is a literal choice between life and death: the preservation of our lives versus the nihilistic death worship of Islam.

Aside from the physical, violent attacks on America and Americans by Islamic jihadists, of equal, if not greater concern to Americans should be the steady abridgement and incremental "repeal" of the First Amendment or freedom of speech by its enemies in our government and by Islamic advocates such as CAIR and its sister entities. This applies to any and all criticism of Islam, whether it is satirical in any form of expression or scholarly or in newsworthy presentations of facts.

If one cannot criticize Islam without expecting a physical attack on one's person, or on an organization such as a publisher, or risking a costly lawsuit by advocates of Islam such as CAIR or the Organization of Islamic Cooperation ("U.S. Praises Sharia Censorship," *The Legal Project*)[58], then one is effectively silenced as though the government had tied a gag over one's mouth or stayed one's pen with fetters or an electronic tracking device.

Without the freedom to speak or write, there is no debate, discourse, criticism or truth-telling, and one is forced to submit to Islam in a state of censorship or coerced ignorance or silence.

The West will be safe from Islamic terrorism only if its politicians and intellectuals reject the *Koran* with its calls for universal slavery and a new Dark Ages, and embrace the *Declaration of Independence*, a magnificent product of the Enlightenment, with its prescription for individual happiness and freedom.

Mr. Cline is the author of the popular *Sparrowhawk* novels, of several detective and suspense novels, and of four anthologies of his commentaries and columns, all available on Amazon Books and Kindle. His articles have appeared, among numerous other publications, in *The Wall Street Journal*, the *Journal of Information Ethics*, and *The Encyclopedia of Library and Information Science*. He is the chief columnist for Rule of Reason, and has contributed featured articles to Family Security Matters, Capitalism Magazine, Breitbart's Big Government, and other Web publications. His special political interests are the First Amendment, freedom of speech, and censorship.

End Notes

1. " Former girlfriend of Boston Bomber reveals he would beat her for dressing like a Westerner and wanted her 'to hate America'," by Hugo Gye. *Daily Mail*, April 29, 2013.

2. "The Violent Quran," by Peter Nilsson. *Dispatch International*, April 19, 2013.

3. "Tamerlan Tsarnaev vowed to die for Islam; judge may have prematurely stopped brother's interrogation, sources say," by Megyn Kelly. *Fox News*, April 25, 2013.

4. "Tsarnaev's Six-Month Visit to Dagestan Is Scrutinized," by Alan Cullison. *The Wall Street Journal*, April 24, 2013.

5. "Canada foils al-Qaeda linked terror plot to derail train," *The Telegraph* (London), April 22, 2013.

6. "Free Speech at Risk: Murder, Mayhem, and Self-Censorship" http://muhammadimages.com/mayhem.php

7. "Terrorist Attacks in the U.S. or Against Americans" http://www.infoplease.com/ipa/A0001454.html#ixzz2S2bKibJa

8. *New World Encyclopedia* on Islam rejecting Enlightenment and reason http://www.newworldencyclopedia.org/entry/Age_of_Enlightenment

9. Ibid, *New World Encyclopedia*

10. "Religious Freedom and a Mosque," on *Political Islam*, by Bill Warner. August 30, 2010 http://www.politicalislam.com/blog/religious-freedom-and-a-mosque

11. "Three Things You (Probably) Didn't Know About Islam." YouTube http://www.youtube.com/watch?v=fgsrnmzxEUY

[12] "Shari'a and Violence in American Mosques," by Mordechai Kedar and David Yerushalmi. *The Middle East Quarterly*, Summer 2011.

[13] *Islamist Watch* on Sharia brutality
http://www.islamist-watch.org/blog/2012/06/life-under-sharia

[14] "CBS Reporter Recounts a 'Merciless' Assault," by Brian Stelter. *The New York Times*, April 28, 2011.

[15] AHA Foundation on honor killings in U.S. and Canada
http://give.theahafoundation.org/blog-0/bid/138443/Forced-Marriage-Honor-Violence-in-the-News

[16] *Fox News* on beheaded wife of Buffalo TV founder
http://www.foxnews.com/story/0,2933,493645,00.html

[17] "American Muslim leader urges faithful to spread Islam's message," by Lisa Gardiner. *San Ramon Valley Herald*, July 4, 1998. PDF of article http://www.anti-cair-net.org/AhmadStateScanned.pdf

[18] "The Muslim Brotherhood's Conquest of Europe," by Lorenzo Vidino. *The Middle East Quarterly*, Winter 2005.

[19] "Turkey's charismatic pro-Islamic leader." *BBC News*, November 4, 2002.

[20] "The Muslim Brotherhood." *Investigative Project on Terrorism*, p. 1.
http://www.investigativeproject.org/documents/misc/135.pdf

[21] "Where is the Muslim Brotherhood Headed?" by Lt. Col. Jonathan D. Halevi. *Jerusalem Center for Public Affairs*, June 20, 2012.

[22] "CounterTerrorism Calendar." National Counterterrorism Center. Hamas http://www.nctc.gov/site/groups/hamas.html

23. "Threat Analysis: Hamas and Hezbollah Sleeper Cells in the United States," by Justin Walker and Leila Golestani, March 18, 2009. *Urban Warfare Analysis Center*, p. 3
http://understandterror.com/articles/Threat%20Analysis%20-%20Hamas%20and%20Hezbollah%20Sleeper%20Cells%20in%20the%20United%20States.pdf

24. "Sleeper Cells in the USA," by Dave Gaubatz. *Family Security Matters*, January 26, 2011.

25. "The Terrorist Network in America, 1991-2007." *Investigative Project on Terrorism*
http://www.investigativeproject.org/maps.php

26. "Correlations Between Sharia Adherence and Violent Dogma in U.S. Mosques," by Mordechai Kedar and David Yerushalmi. *Mapping Shari'a*, Vol. 5, No 5-6 (2011).
http://www.terrorismanalysts.com/pt/index.php/pot/article/view/sharia-adherence-mosque-survey/html

27. Ibid, CounterTerrorism. Al Qaida
http://www.nctc.gov/site/groups/al_qaida.html

28. Ibid., CounterTerrorism. Hizbollah
http://www.nctc.gov/site/groups/hizballah.html

29. Ibid, CounterTerrorism. Taliban
http://www.nctc.gov/site/groups/ttp.html

30. "Pakistan's Osama bin Laden report: al-Qaeda leader feared to set foot outside compound," by Rob Crilly. *The Telegraph* (London), October 21, 2012.

31. "Osama Bin Laden's death: How it happened," by Adrian Brown. *BBC News*, September 10, 2012.

32. "Iran planned Boston bombings for 2 years," by Reza Kahlili. *World News Daily*, April 22, 2013.

33. Ibid.

34. Ibid.

35. "MAS Ducks IPT Questions." *Investigative Project on Terrorism*, August 17, 2010 http://www.investigativeproject.org/2109/mas-ducks-ipt-questions

36. "Russia Repeatedly Warned U.S. About Muslim Boston Bomber," by Daniel Greenfield, *FrontPage*, April 24, 2013.

37. "Mosque that Boston suspects attended has radical ties," by Oren Dorell. *USA TODAY*, April 25, 2013.

38. "On Mosque, Beware the Saudis," by Michael Bard, *The New York Post*, August 22, 2010.

39. Dorell, ibid.

40. Dorell, ibid.

41. "Saudi Publications on Hate Ideology Invade American Mosques." Freedom House, Center for Religious Freedom. P. 17. http://crf.hudson.org/files/publications/SaudiPrcpoganda.pdf

42. Ibid, p. 27.

43. Ibid, p. 7.

44. "Calling Islam 'Islam'," by Bosch Fatwin. *FrontPage*, April 23, 2013.

45. "History of the Muslim Brotherhood Penetration of the U.S. Government," by Clare Lopez. *Gatestone Institute*, April 15, 2013.

46. *Merriam-Webster* definition of nihilism
http://www.merriam-webster.com/dictionary/nihilism

47. *Stanford Encyclopedia of Philosophy* entry on Immanuel Kant
http://plato.stanford.edu/entries/kant-moral/

48. Private correspondence to author, April 22, 2013. See *Muhammad: The Banned Images*
http://muhammadimages.com/

49. "What Does the Religion of Peace Teach About...?" *The Religion of Peace* http://www.thereligionofpeace.com/quran/023-violence.htm

50. "Foreign Terrorist Organizations." Bureau of Counter Terrorism, U.S. Department of State, September 28, 2012
http://www.state.gov/j/ct/rls/other/des/123085.htm

51. "State Sponsors of Terrorism." U.S. Department of State
http://www.state.gov/j/ct/list/c14151.htm

52. John David Lewis, *Nothing Less Than Victory: Decisive Wars and the Lessons of History*. Princeton, NJ: Princeton University Press, 2010. "Victory and the Moral Will to Fight," p. 1.

53. Ibid, pp. 1-2.

54. Ibid, p. 6.

55. "Muslim Brotherhood Explanatory Memorandum." *Investigative Project on Terrorism*. P. 21
http://www.investigativeproject.org/documents/case_docs/445.pdf

56. "End States Who Sponsor Terrorism," by Dr. Leonard Peikoff
http://www.peikoff.com/essays_and_articles/end-states-who-sponsor-terrorism/

[57] "John Brennan: From Mecca to Washington,' by Daniel Greenfield. *FrontPage*, February 18, 2013.

[58] "U.S. Praises Sharia Censorship," by Deborah Weiss. *The Legal Project*, May 24, 2013.
http://www.legal-project.org/4088/us-praises-sharia-censorship

Postscript

Since the original publication of *Islam's Reign of Terror* by Voltaire Press in 2013, scores of acts of terror have been committed overseas, in the Mideast, and numerous acts committed in the United States, including the Boston Marathon bombing of April 15th, 2013, by two Islamic Chechen brothers. Many would-be domestic Islamic terrorists have been foiled by our hamstrung authorities and arrested. Israel was attacked by Hamas, which was provisionally defeated after the terrorist "government" of Gaza launched thousands of rockets at Israeli population centers. Israel discovered a maze of tunnels emanating from Gaza into Israel, built chiefly with "humanitarian" supplies, such as cement and steel, from Israel and other nations. The tunnel complex was supposed to have enabled Hamas to launch a mass raid on Israel with the purpose of killing thousands of Israelis during a Jewish holiday. Hamas has broken several ceasefires, renewing its rocket attacks.

To be more accurate, nearly 26,000* acts of terror in the name of Islam, have been carried out in the U.S. and worldwide including the ones listed earlier in this pamphlet. These number in the thousands. A Boston jury has found Dzhokhar Tsarnaev, one of the Boston Marathon bombers, guilty and sentenced him to death. More recently, earlier in 2015, the French satirical magazine, Charlie Hebdo, was attacked by Islamic terrorists for caricaturing Mohammad, and twelve staffers killed. And in Garland, Texas, May 3rd, the Draw Mohammad contest event was attacked, but was foiled by a single policeman, who shot and killed the two gunmen. They were the only "casualties."

Most recently, a new terrorist organization, ISIS, or the Islamic State of Iraq and Syria (or, variously, the Islamic State of Syria and the Levant, or ISL), has emerged and conquered wide swathes of Syria and Iraq. ISIS has killed thousands of Christians, Shi'ites, and members of other religious sects, such as the Yazidis, captured hundreds of non-Sunni women as "sex slaves," and displaced thousands more in its drive to Baghdad to establish a caliphate. ISIS has vowed to carry its terrorism to the U.S. and other Western nations. Western, including U.S., response to the threat has been desultory, at best. Indeed, ISIS is alleged to have been present during the Ferguson, Missouri race riots of August this year. In the meantime, countless Muslim "citizens" of various European countries or residing in the West have traveled to Syria to join the *jihad* against the Syrian and other governments. Their return to Europe and America, armed with new terrorist skills, poses an especially perilous danger.

Finally, the mass, uncontrolled immigration of Mexicans and Central Americans over the U.S.-Mexican border into the U.S. has also enabled the stealth infiltration by *jihadists* into the U.S., posing as Hispanics, from the Mideast and Africa.

§   The End   §

* The Religion of Peace, May 19th, 2015
at http://www.thereligionofpeace.com/

Islam's Reign of Terror

www.ingramcontent.com/pod-product-compliance
Lightning Source LLC
Chambersburg PA
CBHW060220290526
45789CB00003B/1342